# THE IMMUTABILITY OF GOD'S COUNSEL

# The Immutability of God's Counsel

## ...with 50 Promises of God according to His Infallible Word.

ANTHONY ADEFARAKAN

GLOEM, CANADA

# CONTENTS

~ ~

Introduction

1

~ ~

Fifty (50) Promises of God according to His Infallible Word.

3

~ ~

Conclusion

11

~ ~

Become a Financial Partner with Jesus

13

~ ~

About the Author

15

# INTRODUCTION

Hebrews 6:13-17 (NKJV) says:

"For when God made a promise to Abraham, because He could swear by no one greater, He swore by Himself, saying 'Surely blessing I will bless you, and multiplying I will multiply you'. And so, after he had patiently endured, he obtained the promise. For men indeed swear by the greater, and an oath for confirmation is for them an end of all dispute. Thus God, determining to show more abundantly to the heirs of promise the immutability of His counsel, confirmed it by an oath, that by two immutable things, in which it is impossible for God to lie, we might have strong consolation, who have fled for refuge to lay hold of the hope set before us."

When a promise is made, one may be doubtful as to whether the fellow making the promise will fulfill it or not; but when the fellow backs up the promise with an oath – swearing by someone greater than himself, every form of doubt will disappear because the fellow is now bound to fulfill what he has promised. This was the case with God and Abraham. He gave him a promise, and since there is no one greater than Him, He decided to swear by Himself. He put His Almightiness, Holiness, Righteousness, Most Highness and Sovereignty on the line; and sure enough, He fulfilled what He promised him – He blessed him and greatly multiplied him.

The text says God is determined to show to us too being the heirs of the promise He made to our father Abraham the immutability of His counsel so that we can be rest assured that what He has promised us, He will surely fulfill if only we will exhibit faith and patience as our father did – verses 15-17.

The word 'immutability' according to Oxford Advanced Learner's Dictionary means something that cannot be changed, something that will never change. That's what God is trying to get across. Since He will never tell a lie (Numbers 23:19), He is saying He will fulfill all He has promised us, without changing any of them. This is because He had sworn by Himself to do so.

This book in your hand is a collection of fifty (50) of the promises He had made to all His children; as you read and meditate on them, ask Him to fulfill them in your own life and He will definitely do so.

Anthony Adefarakan

# FIFTY (50) PROMISES OF GOD ACCORDING TO HIS INFALLIBLE WORD.

1. **Isaiah 55:5**
   "Surely you shall call a nation you do not know, and nations who do not know you shall run to you, because of the LORD your God, and the Holy One of Israel; for He has glorified you."

2. **Isaiah 58:11**
   "The LORD will guide you continually, and satisfy your soul in drought, and strengthen your bones; you shall be like a watered garden, and like a spring of water, whose waters do not fail."

3. **Isaiah 54:4**
   "Do not fear, for you will not be ashamed, nor be disgraced, for you will not be put to shame; for you will forget the shame of your youth; and will not remember the reproach of your widowhood anymore".

4. **Isaiah 54: 13-14**
   "All your children shall be taught by the LORD, and great shall be the peace of you children. In righteousness you shall be established; you shall be far from oppression, for you shall not fear, and from terror, for it shall not come near you."

5. **Isaiah 54:17a**

    "No weapon formed against you shall prosper, and every tongue which rises against you in judgment you shall condemn."

6. **Isaiah 43:2**

    "When you pass through the waters, I will be with you; and through the rivers, they shall not overflow you. When you walk through the fire, you shall not be burned, nor shall the flame scorch you."

7. **Isaiah 43:18-19**

    "Do not remember the former things, nor consider the things of old. Behold, I will do a new thing; now it shall spring forth; shall you not know it? I will even make a road in the wilderness and rivers in the desert."

8. **Job 8:7**

    "Though your beginning was small, yet your latter end would increase abundantly."

9. **Job 8:22a**

    "Those who hate you will be clothed with shame..."

10. **Psalm 32:8**

    "I will instruct you and teach you in the way you should go; I will guide you with My eye."

11. **Isaiah 30:21**

    "Your ears shall hear a word behind you, saying, 'This is the way, walk in it', whenever you turn to the right hand or whenever you turn to the left."

12. **Isaiah 49:15-16**

    "Can a woman forget her nursing child, and not have compassion on the son of her womb? Surely they may forget, yet I will not forget you. See, I have inscribed you on the palms of My hands; your walls are continually before Me."

13. **Isaiah 49:24-26**

    "Shall the prey be taken from the mighty, or the captives of the righteous be delivered? But thus says the LORD; 'Even the captives of the mighty shall be taken away, and the prey of the terrible be delivered; for I will contend with him who contends with you, and I will save your children. I will feed those who oppress you with their own flesh, and they shall be drunk with their own blood as with sweet wine. All flesh shall know that I, the LORD, am your Savior and your Redeemer, the Mighty One of Jacob."

14. **Isaiah 66:9**

    "'Shall I bring to the time of birth, and not cause delivery?' says the LORD. 'Shall I who cause delivery shut up the womb?' says your God."

15. **Jeremiah 1:8**

    "Do not be afraid of their faces, for I am with you to deliver you; says the LORD."

16. **Joshua 1:3a**

    "Every place that the sole of your foot will tread upon I have given you…"

17. **Joshua 1:9**

    "Have I not commanded you? Be strong and of good courage; do not be afraid, nor be dismayed, for the LORD your God is with you wherever you go."

18. **Jeremiah 1:19**

    "They will fight against you, but they shall not prevail against you. For I am with you, says the LORD, to deliver you."

19. **Jeremiah 29:11-12**

    "For I know the thoughts that I think toward you, says the LORD, 'thoughts of peace and not of evil, to give you a future and a hope.' Then, you will call upon Me and go and pray to Me, and I will listen to you."

20. **Jeremiah 31:17a**

    "'There is hope in your future,' says the LORD."

21. **Jeremiah 33:3**
    "Call to Me, and I will answer you, and show you great and mighty things, which you do not know."

22. **Ezekiel 12:25,28**
    "For I am the LORD, I speak, and the word which I speak will come to pass; it will no more be postponed; for in your days...I will say the word and perform it; says the Lord God."
    "...Thus says the Lord God, 'None of My words will be postponed any more, but the word which I speak will be done', says the Lord God."

23. **Ezekiel 18:21**
    "But if a wicked man turns from all his sins which he has committed, keeps all My statutes, and does what is lawful and right, he shall surely live; he shall not die."

24. **Joel 2:26**
    "You shall eat in plenty and be satisfied, and praise the name of the LORD your God, who has dealt wondrously with you; and My people shall never be put to shame."

25. **Nahum 1:9**
    "What do you conspire against the LORD? He will make an utter end of it. Affliction will not rise up a second time."

26. **Zephaniah 3:19**
    "Behold, at that time, I will deal with all who afflict you; I will save the lame, and gather those who were driven out; I will appoint them for praise and fame in every land where they were put to shame."

27. **Zechariah 1:3**
    "...Thus says the LORD of hosts; Return to Me, says the LORD of hosts, and I will return to you, says the LORD of hosts."

28. **Malachi 3:6**
"For I am the LORD, I do not change; therefore you are not consumed, O sons of Jacob."

29. **Malachi 4:2**
"But to you who fear My name the Sun of Righteousness shall arise with healing in His wings; and you shall go out and grow fat like stall – fed calves."

30. **Isaiah 3:10**
"Say to the righteous that it shall be well with them, for they shall eat the fruit of their doings."

31. **2 Chronicles 7:14**
"If My people who are called by My name will humble themselves, and pray and seek My face and turn from their wicked ways, then I will hear from heaven, and will forgive their sin and heal their land."

32. **Genesis 12:2-3**
"I will make you a great nation; I will bless you and make your name great; and you shall be a blessing. I will bless those who bless you, and I will curse him who curses you; and in you all the families of the earth shall be blessed."

33. **Matthew 18:18-19**
"Assuredly, I say to you, whatever you bind on earth will be bound in heaven, and whatever you loose on earth will be loosed in heaven. Again, I say to you that if two of you agree on earth concerning anything that they shall ask, it will be done for them by My Father in heaven."

34. **Matthew 19:29**
"And everyone who has left houses or brothers or sisters or father or mother or wife or children or lands for My name's sake shall receive a hundredfold, and inherit everlasting life."

35. **Matthew 21:22**

    "And all things, whatever you ask in prayer, believing, you will receive."

36. **Matthew 24:35**

    "Heaven and earth will pass away, but My words will by no means pass away."

37. **Matthew 28:20b**

    "I am with you always, even to the end of the age."

38. **Luke 11:13**

    "If you then, being evil, know how to give good gifts to your children, how much more will your heavenly Father give the Holy Spirit to those who ask Him!"

39. **John 6:37**

    "All that the Father gives Me will come to Me, and the one who comes to Me I will by no means cast out."

40. **John 7:38**

    "He who believes in Me, as the Scripture has said, out of his heart will flow rivers of living water."

41. **John 12:26**

    "If anyone serves Me, let him follow Me; and where I am, there My servant will be also. If anyone serves Me, him My Father will honor."

42. **John 14:26**

    "But the Helper, the Holy Spirit, whom the Father will send in My name, He will teach you all things, and bring to your remembrance all things that I said to you."

43. **John 15:17**

    "If you abide in Me, and My words abide in you, you will ask what you desire; and it shall be done for you."

44. **John 16:33**

    "These things I have spoken to you, that in Me you may have peace. In the world you will have tribulation; but be of good cheer, I have overcome the world."

45. **Matthew 7:7**
"Ask, and it will be given to you; seek, and you will find; knock, and it will be opened to you."

46. **James 1:5**
"If any of you lacks wisdom, let him ask of God, who gives to all liberally and without reproach, and it will be given to him."

47. **Revelation 3:20**
"Behold, I stand at the door and knock. If anyone hears My voice and opens the door, I will come in to him and dine with him and he with Me."

48. **Isaiah 40:29**
"He gives power to the weak, and to those who have no might He increases strength."

49. **Isaiah 41:10,13**
"Fear not, for I am with you; be not dismayed, for I am your God; I will strengthen you, yes I will help you, I will uphold you with My righteous right hand. For I, the LORD your God, will hold your right hand, saying to you, 'Fear not, I will help you.'"

50. **Revelation 22:12**
"And behold, I am coming quickly, and My reward is with Me, to give everyone according to his work."

## CONCLUSION

These promises are meant to be claimed because they are actually ours as God's children. As regards their fulfillment, Numbers 23:19 has taken care of that. It says 'God is not a man that He should lie; neither the son of man that He should repent; hath He said, and shall He not do it? or hath He spoken, and shall He not make good?'

So we can be sure that He will do what He has promised.

However, these promises may not be fulfilled in a person's life if such a person starts dishonoring or disregarding the One who made the promises. A very good example is in 1 Samuel 2:30; "Therefore the LORD God of Israel says: 'I said indeed that your house and the house of your father would walk before Me forever;' but now the LORD says: Far be it from Me; for those who honor Me I will honor, and those who despise Me shall be lightly esteemed."

You see, it is a very terrible thing to have God withdraw His good promises from an individual. Eli did not respect God and he lost those beautiful promises.

In this dispensation, the greatest honor you can give to God is to gladly accept His precious and sacrificial Gift to humanity – His only begotten Son, Jesus Christ. Accepting Jesus Christ into your life is the greatest of all the honor you can give to God; and with Jesus, all of God's promises are surely going to be fulfilled in your life.

If you are willing to do that now, you can quickly say this prayer:

*"Lord Jesus, I am a sinner. Please have mercy on me and cleanse me by Your precious Blood of atonement. Kindly erase my name from the book of death and write it in the Book of Life. I accept You as my*

*<u>personal Lord and Saviour; and by Your grace, I promise to live the rest of my life bringing You glory. Thank You for saving me."</u>*

Yes, you are now qualified to enjoy the fulfillment of all the good promises God has made concerning you in His Word. Start claiming them now; they will be fulfilled in your life and you will praise the Lord. Hallelujah!

# BECOME A FINANCIAL PARTNER WITH JESUS

At *Global Emancipation Ministries - Calgary*, our mandate is *to liberate men through the knowledge of the Truth* and our mission statement is *creating channels through which men can encounter the Truth [Isaiah 61:1-3; John 8:32, 36; I Thessalonians 5:24]*.

**Our Ministerial Activities include** Rural and Urban Evangelical Outreaches, Prison Evangelism, Hospital Ministrations, Mobilization for Missions Support, Teaching of the undiluted Word of God, Scripture-Based Seminars, Discipleship, Training of Field Missionaries and Empowerment of underprivileged ones among other Field Ministerial Tasks.

If you sense the Lord is calling you to reach out to the lost by engaging in any of these activities or by assisting those involved with your resources, please feel free to join us. Let us come together as we take the Gospel of our Lord Jesus Christ to the hurting and forgotten ones.

[Mark 16:15-20].

Please join us in these kingdom projects by making your weekly, monthly, quarterly or annual donations to Global Emancipation Ministries – Calgary.

You can visit the "GIVE" section on our website, www.gloem.org, to learn about other ways to give.

For acknowledgement, please advise your donations to us by email: info@gloem.org or emancipation4souls@yahoo.com, and kindly include your details i.e. name, address, email and location. Alternatively, you can simply call +1 587 9735910 to do same.

You can also volunteer your gifts and talents in the service of the Lord through our ministerial platforms regardless of your location. To get information on how to go about this, please visit www.gloem.org and contact us via email: info@gloem.org or emancipation4souls@yahoo.com.

God bless you.

# ABOUT THE AUTHOR

By the special grace of God, **Anthony O. Adefarakan** is the privileged President of **Global Emancipation Ministries - Calgary (GLOEM)** with headquarters in Canada, North America and **Emancipating Truth Ministry International (ETMI)** with headquarters in Nigeria, West Africa.

The Lord called him into the field ministry in February 2008 with the mandate to liberate men through the knowledge of the Truth, and by December 2012 he was ordained and commissioned as the Pioneer Pastor – in – Charge of The Redeemed Christian Church of God, Revelation Parish, Shalom Area under Delta Province III, Nigeria where he served until 1st February 2015 when he officially handed over to a new Pastor in order to focus on his field ministry to which the Lord had earlier called him and for which the authority of the church had already prayed and released him to undertake.

On 29th September 2013, he was awarded a Post Graduate Diploma in Tent – Making Mission from the Redeemed Christian School of Missions, Nigeria (RECSOM, Asaba Campus) where he also had the privilege to train Pastors and Missionaries as a lecturer in 2017.

Since the commissioning of his field ministry in 2015 he has had the opportunity to lead his ministry officers to field ministrations in different Prisons, Hospitals, Orphanages, Rural communities, Camp settlements, Markets, Local churches among other places with great successes on all occasions – such as salvation of sinners, healing of the sick, financial empowerment of mission churches, provision of relief materials to the poor, provision of medical services to the underprivileged, baptism in the Holy Ghost, deliverance from demonic oppression, release of inmates just to mention a few - all to the glory of God Who alone is the Doer.

He is the author of other best-selling titles such as ***The Law of Kinds, It's Your Size, The Immutability of God's Counsel, Surely there is an End, Life Applicable lessons from the Book of Ruth, One thing is Needful, Life Applicable Revelations from God's Word*** among others.

He is happily married to Ifeoluwa A. Adefarakan and their marriage is fruitful to the glory of God.

**Jesus is his Message, Freedom is the Outcome!**
**Isaiah 61:1-3**

www.ingramcontent.com/pod-product-compliance
Lightning Source LLC
Chambersburg PA
CBHW042235090526
44589CB00001B/12